This Journal Belongs To

_____

_____

_____

For other products with this and other designs,
please visit us at our Etsy shop.
www.nimblemuseprintables.etsy.com

For questions and/or concerns, contact us at
nimblemuse@gmail.com

If you have enjoyed this publication and found it useful, we would
be grateful if you would leave us a review.
Thank you.

Made in the USA
Middletown, DE
27 April 2023

29557267R00071